The West Highland Way with a Wheelchair

by
Sandy Gibson

Who, together with John Bell, took on the mighty West Highland Way!

AuthorHouse™
1663 Liberty Drive, Suite 200
Bloomington, IN 47403
www.authorhouse.com
Phone: 1-800-839-8640

© 2009 Sandy Gibson. All rights reserved.

No part of this book may be reproduced, stored in a retrieval system, or transmitted by any means without the written permission of the author.

First published by AuthorHouse 11/23/2009

ISBN: 978-1-4389-5192-8 (sc)

Printed in the United States of America
Bloomington, Indiana

This book is printed on acid-free paper.

For my darling John, who never lost faith in me, even when I did!

Also for Chris, without whom this book would never have come to fruition.

The West Highland Way with a Wheelchair

For many years, I ran a poodle parlour and pet shop, running up and down to the flat above the shop with 20kilo sacks of dog food. In 1997 I started to notice that my legs were getting tired and I was puffed-out half way up the stairs. I stopped smoking in January 1998, thinking that this was the culprit, but it had no effect. I'd been a member of Mensa - the club for people with high IQs - for many years, and had recently started going to games evenings again after a break of several years. There I had met John Bell. Telling him about my lack of energy, he suggested that I go swimming with him to try and get fit, and also for the occasional walk with the intention of eventually joining a rambling club.

I was still tripping up and losing balance for no apparent reason, and during the next few years made several fruitless visits to the doctor with varying symptoms. I even suggested that it might be Multiple Sclerosis; but in the end, the doctor obviously thought I was a hypochondriac and insisted that it was just 'wear and tear'. Eventually in desperation I changed my doctor. Although the new doctor didn't think it was anything to worry about - and certainly not MS- at least she took my concerns seriously and arranged for me to see a specialist. The specialist also reassured me that it wouldn't be anything serious; he said it would probably be 'one of those things we never get to the bottom of', which I guessed referred to ME or 'Yuppy Flu'. However, he arranged an MRI scan, which, to his surprise showed 'lesions' on the spine.

Things moved fairly fast after this, and I spent two days in hospital having a battery of tests, including a lumbar puncture. That was it, a diagnosis at last; it was 2001 by this time. The reason the doctors had refused to believe I had MS, I discovered a while later. Reading an article in an MS magazine, I found a description of my symptoms exactly, and discovered I had a rare form of MS called Primary Progressive. This explained why I had never had a 'relapse' and couldn't identify with anything I had previously read about MS; although I had thought the symptoms similar enough to suspect I had it. In the article; it was described as 'The worse sort of MS', but certainly in my case, I find it a lot easier to handle than having relapses at unknown intervals. At least I know roughly how I'll be in a year's time for instance, and can make plans ahead. It's difficult to explain to people who ask me if I was devastated at the diagnosis; that no, actually I felt a tremendous sense of relief; that at last I knew what I was dealing with, and could carry on with my life accordingly.

I was finding it increasingly difficult to manage at work; it was a very physical job, and when my assistant gave in her notice, I realized that it was impossible to carry on alone. As I was over sixty anyway, I decided it was time to hang up my clippers. So in October 2002 I became a pensioner. Then two months later, three days before Christmas, my husband came home from the bowls club to which he belonged, and, as I was chatting to him while he opened a Christmas present he had brought home with him, he suddenly collapsed with a heart attack. By the time the paramedics arrived, he was dead. Watching the person one loves best dying in front of one is an horrendous experience, but at least I had the comfort of knowing that he didn't suffer.

So there it was; in the course of just over a year, I'd been diagnosed with MS, had to retire and lost my much - loved husband. Needless to say, I felt as though the rug had been pulled out from under my feet; the house felt as though it had died as well. When talking to my brother on the phone soon afterwards, I told him how the heart had gone from the house, and he advised me not to do anything drastic, like moving, as the house would recover with time, it would be slightly different, but would get its heart back.

Physically it took its toll as well; I developed Shingles, Tonsillitis and a water infection, all at the same time, and after crawling back from the chemist with some antibiotics one day, I took to my bed. When John came round to take me swimming the next morning, I'd given up and couldn't even open my eyes. Thank goodness for John; he took a day off work and got me mobile again and functioning fairly normally. Each time I had a particularly bad day, he'd take time off work and drive me all over the countryside, buying me lunch on the way; but I'll never forget the dreadful feeling of loss and unreality that consumed my whole being at that time.

In August 2003, just eight months later, my dear old cat Pebbles died and left me totally alone. I'd reached rock bottom, and found it extremely hard to 'think positively'; my bereavement counsellor said one day "You're going to have to think about moving on with your life." I replied; "I've got an incurable illness, have had to give up my business, have lost my husband and my last remaining pet has died; I feel as though the rug has been pulled out from under me; where is it I'm supposed to move on TO?" She thought for a moment and then said "Yes, I see your point."

On the advice of my daughter I joined a singles club and started going out socially. As she pointed out, I could either sit at home feeling sorry for myself, or get out and start to live again. I went to a few meetings; had a weekend away at a park centre in Cumbria, where I felt intensely lonely and cut off, as I was not able to join in with most able bodied activities; and I met a couple of chaps socially. Meeting a lady member for lunch one day, I commented that although I had met these two blokes, I had found that I had no inclination to take the relationships any further; to which she replied "No, of course you won't while you're in love with someone else." On seeing my puzzled expression, she pointed out that I'd mentioned John every second sentence, and it was absolutely obvious that I was besotted with him. Anyway, to cut a long story short, I'd gradually been caring more and more for him, and, for his part, he'd been in love with me for quite a while and unbeknownst to me had become increasingly worried that I'd meet someone else and he'd lose me. So he panicked, and turned up on my doorstep with a suitcase one evening! Although I was pretty worried about this turn of events, because I didn't think I was anywhere near ready for another relationship, it has worked extraordinarily well, mainly because we were such good friends already, with a lot in common. All of a sudden it became easy to "Think positively", and my house has become a warm and cosy home once again.

John belonged to a rambling club, and was used to going off every Sunday walking with them. The first two Sundays that he was with me, he went off as usual, but we missed each other so much that he said he wasn't going any more. This made me feel very guilty, as I knew how much he enjoyed his walking. So I suggested that he just push me round the streets in my wheelchair for exercise. The walks tended to expand beyond streets; and in the middle of winter, struggling over a frosty ploughed field (impossible to push the chair with me in it), wearing a pair of pink suede shoes (me, not him!) was not ideal! Walking on rough ground was also very difficult for me; on pavements I could push the wheelchair, which gave me something to hold on to, but on rough terrain I couldn't manage the chair, and staggered about tripping and swearing. Then one day, walking along the scarp by the 'white horse' near Sutton Bank, (a well known beauty spot with a visitor centre), we met a woman coming the other way with two spiked sticks that looked rather like ski sticks. I commented "Now THAT'S what I could do with", whereupon she stopped and showed me how they adjusted to any length, and said that they had made a fantastic difference to her. We bought some as soon as we could, following which John bought me some walking boots and bit by bit I acquired most of the clothes and accessories available for walking in any weather. Walking was no longer an ordeal, but something I could enjoy come rain or shine. I picked up a very nice padded jacket with both Velcro and a zip, and also a body warmer to go under it, both from charity shops.

We took a weekend break in Glasgow; where John grew up; and while there we went for a visit to Loch Lomond. John showed me where the West Highland Way ran past the hotel where we had lunch. "Don't you fancy having a go at it?" he asked "You must be joking!" was my horrified reply.

It took John about two years to talk me into attempting this mad idea, but once decided upon, it took over our every waking thought! John got in touch with Easyways; a marvellous company who did all the booking for us, including arranging for Travel-Lite to ferry our luggage from hotel to hotel. What wonderful firms these are; they take all the worry out of the preparations, and are so friendly and helpful.

Once the trains were booked, we were free to concentrate on the training. We booked with Easyways in December, so there was plenty of time to try out various terrains in different weather conditions. We did one particular walk in torrential rain and thank goodness we did, because it proved that my coat may have been shower proof, but it certainly wasn't heavy rain proof; the only parts of me that were dry were my feet. Also, John's waterproof trousers - weren't! Off to the shop for a super "Kag in a Bag" for me and new trousers for John. The next walk we did was on the Yorkshire moors in a snow blizzard; oh how cosy I felt. We also tried some really steep rocky climbs; these gave me an inkling of how I'd manage on the deadly 'Devil's Staircase'. I found that when my legs got really tired, a few minutes rest enabled me to continue for a while. Oh, how it took up our thoughts and discussions; I was so worried about letting John down; but he said that even if I didn't finish it, the fact that I'd tried was enough.

The NHS had kindly supplied a light - weight wheelchair, which we tested very thoroughly beforehand. I had it serviced just before we left, and as the front wheels were a little battered by that time, the chap replaced them with new ones and gave me the old ones as spares.

At the Stockton MS group where I am a member, several people had asked if I was getting sponsorship. I hadn't thought about it before; and wasn't sure whether to or not; but as June, the lady who does all the treatments at the centre (such as massage, manicure, reflexology etc.) pointed out, it'd be an awful waste if I didn't use the opportunity to raise a little money for our group. So I decided to go ahead with the idea and obtained some sponsorship forms. June also gave me some massage oils for my legs, with instructions how to mix them. John should massage my legs each night after walking, she told me, and that would help me to keep supple and pain free. Hotels were booked, trains were booked, the baggage carrier was booked, that was about it, and we were ready to roll!

I made a long list of items for packing, we took one large case and one smaller one with changes of clothes, toiletries, medicines and all the etceteras that one usually has to take on a holiday, but I also made a list of items to pack in the rucksack. These were things that we needed to take with us on the actual walk; water bottle, camera, waterproofs, rope (which John said we wouldn't need, but proved vital later on), maps, satellite navigation system, sun lotion and various other essentials. However, we took care not to pack anything surplus to requirements, as space was at a premium and weight was very important. One thing

I overlooked though, was a sun hat; we had prepared so much in anticipation of the worst weather that apart from sun cream, I'd not really packed for good conditions. My spiked sticks were sitting happily in a firmly fixed stick holder on the wheelchair and a spare wheel was clamped underneath with cable ties. The other spare wheel we packed in the case.

STARTING OUT

John insisted we walk the first leg of the journey to Billingham station. Start as we mean to go on was his philosophy, which wouldn't have been so bad if we hadn't had two heavy bags to carry, as well as the rucksack and wheelchair. The bag which I'd considered the 'small' bag, turned out to be extremely heavy, as for some reason it had a removable bottom which was made of metal which is definitely coming off next time.

We had to negotiate the bridge at the unmanned station, after walking there with the large bag on my lap, and the smaller one slung over John's shoulder. We had to change trains at Newcastle and again at Motherwell and had booked assistance at both. We had a laugh with the guard at Motherwell, because the door to the cupboard where the ramps were stored wouldn't shut properly, and he had quite a job with it, making uncomplimentary comments about new trains as he struggled. When we got to Milngavie (pronounced Millguy), the guard couldn't open the cupboard door, so we climbed off under our own steam.

Leaving home

Walking to station

Milngavie Station

Unfortunately, the strap on the smaller bag snapped soon after leaving Milngavie station for the ten minute walk to the hotel. We were struggling along with both bags on my lap, which meant that I couldn't see a thing, when a very kind Scottish lady insisted on carrying the smaller bag, (which incidentally was very heavy) all the way to the hotel! I was getting increasingly nervous as she first told us that she'd tried the West Highland Way with her husband, and had given up after two days, because she was so unfit, then went on to say that she'd recently collapsed at work! As she was getting redder and redder in the face, but firmly refusing to relinquish the bag, I was extremely relieved to reach the hotel. She did however tell us a very amusing anecdote, about how on the second day, her husband had stopped to relieve himself against a fence, finding out too late that it was electrified!

We stayed at the Premier Inn in Milngavie, which was a very nice hotel, with pleasant staff, if a little impersonal. The food was served next door and was excellent, catering for vegetarians with a very nice nut cutlet.

Gilbert of Travel-Lite

The next morning, after having had my legs crushed the previous day, we put the bags on the chair and I walked to the Travel-Lite van, and the start of the West Highland Way. Gilbert, from Travel-Lite, was very helpful and offered to pick me up if we got stuck at any point. "Not you though," he said to John, "There's only room for one!"

We left our bags in Gilbert's capable hands and made our way to the obelisk which marks the beginning of the Way. This is quite odd, as it is situated right in the middle of a shopping precinct.

We took our photo and one for a couple of foreign girls who were just starting out also, and away we went, following the route which is clearly marked with posts decorated with carved thistles.

Starting point

MILNGAVIE TO DRYMEN (12 MILES)

Our first day started out sunny and after following a path by a river, we wound our way upwards out of Milngavie. It was a fairly steep grassy slope, but didn't seem too hard to climb, (although I did have to do my first stint at walking with my spiked sticks,) and we were amazed when we turned round at the top, to see how far above Milngavie we had come.

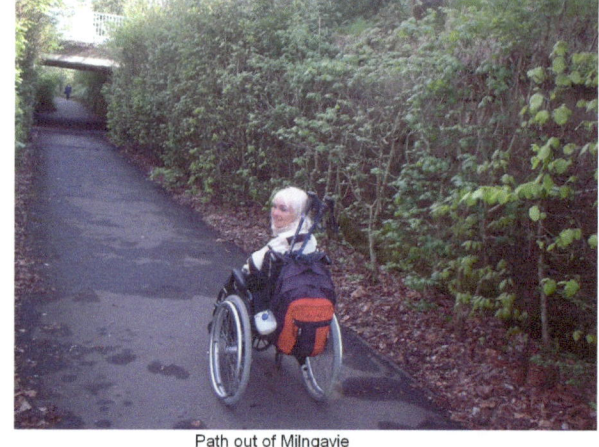

We were caught up by a friendly retriever called Darcy, who had rushed ahead of two ladies to say hello to us.

Path out of Milngavie

We went on a bit further and were chatting to a couple of walkers coming the other way, when it started to spit with rain. As we went along by some little holiday chalets, a very friendly cat came over to talk to us, and at that point it started to rain quite heavily, so on went the waterproofs.

The first serious obstacle we met was a stone wall with staggered stones sticking out up to the top, to use as steps. I had very little problem with it, but it wasn't easy to get the chair over. As we carried on, the way got more rugged, and my sticks came into play again. We were met by Darcy and his two friends, one of the ladies said that they were on their way back now as they had children to pick up. "We went as far as the Beech Tree, so you haven't long to go for a drink." One commented, which was very cheering news.

Dog called Darcy

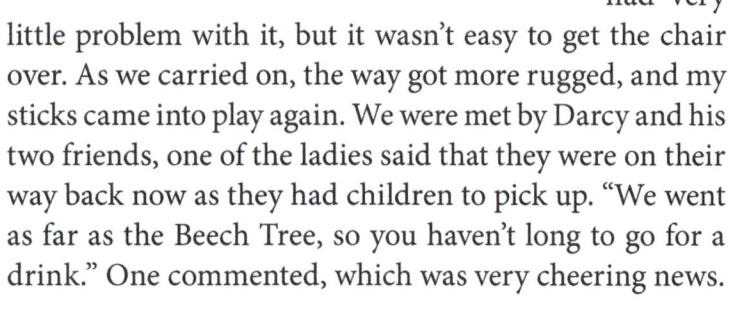

Unknown pussy cat

There were a few styles to negotiate, but nothing hard and we walked along a disused railway until we got to The Beech Tree Inn for a very welcome lunch, with of course the obligatory couple of pints. It was a lovely old inn, with a pagoda outside for rucksacks and sticks etc. and whilst there, we saw the couple of girls whose picture we had taken at the obelisk.

Winnock Hotel in Drymen

Inside Winnock Hotel

After lunch we continued along the disused railway for quite a way. Some showers again, but nothing very heavy. We encountered some stone steps with no hand rail and then some rickety steps up to a long country road, with many ups and downs. We climbed a very steep grass hill which had the thistle sign on a post at the top. After crossing a couple of muddy fields and a main road, we walked down a small road into Drymen and the Winnock hotel.

The hotel was gorgeous, very old with a stag's head over a roaring fire in a large hearth. We were allowed to have dinner in front of the fire, and would have sat there longer, but I didn't feel too good, with a blinding headache, so we went up to bed early.

I woke at ten thirty with stomach cramps, and lay listening to a strange rumbling noise that was getting louder. The noise woke John and we decided it must be thunder. John went to the bathroom and whilst he was in there, there was an almighty crack which made me jump out of my skin. I shouted "That was right overhead; in fact I wouldn't be surprised to find that something near had been struck by lighting." In the morning the Manager glumly told us that the back roof had been struck!

Drymen to Rowardennan (14 miles)

I was very relieved to find that my upset tummy and headache of the night before seemed to have settled down for the time being, and after a light breakfast we set off for Rowardenan.

We soon had our first view of Loch Lomond, and looked back at the small mountain Dumgoyne, which John remembered climbing as a Boy Scout many years before.

The day was dry and sunny, if a little coolish. It was a very pleasant forestry walk and when we got to Conic Hill, which was a very steep and rocky climb, I must admit I was quite relieved to find notices saying that lambing was in progress and we must go round by the road. The small streams were all full of water from the storm of the night before. The wild flowers were wonderful; I've never seen so many primroses, and mixed with them were bluebells and some white flowers I didn't know the name of, the path sides were an absolute picture.

Path out of Drymen

First view of Loch Lomond

When we got to the road with traffic on, it was pavemented all the way, and a toot on a horn made us look round. There was Gilbert on his way to Rowardenan with our bags!

We walked some of the way with a very nice couple called Barbara and Bob, and their small border collie Billie. We had to wait in places as cars went by, as there were large

Road to Balmaha

puddles, and as the traffic went past, it was throwing water all over the pavement. We stopped for beer and lunch in Balmaha at a lovely old Inn called the Oak Tree, and saw the first ash trays of the trip! They were on the tables in the garden. The no smoking law means that all the pubs and hotels smell fresh; it'll be lovely when the same law comes into force in England.

The path from Balmaha was rather broken in places with a few ups and downs, a slight foretaste of what was to come.

The Oak Tree in Balmaha

Loch Lomond shore at Balmaha

Loch side after leaving Balmaha

Resting on path to Rowardennan

Loch Lomond side

11

Negotiating small stream

A bridge on the way to Rowardennan

Steep part of path to Rowardennan

Crossing drainage ditch

More climbing

Primroses growing at the side of the path

We reached Rowardenan at 6.30pm, and were given a lovely room with a window overlooking the loch.

View from window in Rowardennan hotel

Sadly, as well as my tummy playing up again during the night, there was a karate club staying, and they woke us up at 12.30am, and again at 2.30am, banging on doors and shouting at their friends to wake up. I got very mad and shouted back that everyone WAS awake! They seemed to quieten down after that, in the morning Barbara and Bob, who were staying at the same hotel, complained to the manager, but it was too late for us. The hotel had made us a packed lunch, as there were no inns on the next day's walk, and we bought some postcards.

We'd heard some pretty bad things about the next two phases and as Barbara and Bob were going on ahead of us; doing two phases together in one day; we asked Barbara to text back what the next stage was like.

Rowardennan to Inversnaid (7.25 miles)

As Inversnaid is about a hundred miles round trip by road, Travel-Lite doesn't visit there with the bags, but goes straight on to the next hotel; because of this we had to carry the barest essentials with us.

The first part of this section was hilly, but a very good track; the second part was not so hilly, but was uneven and difficult. We stopped for lunch on a bench overlooking the loch.

Crossing a gate on way to Inversnaid

Path from Rowardennan to Inversnaid

Small waterfall

Pushing wheelchair up a slope

View across Loch Lomond

Rough path along loch side

Lunch beside the loch

The next section will live in my memory for the rest of my life! We were clambering along a steep rocky path with a sheer drop on the left side down to the loch, when John exclaimed in a shocked tone. I can't remember what he said, if anything, but the high rock on the right curved round to the right and as we came round the bend, we were faced with a rock ledge about a foot wide, with a steep craggy drop on the left and a wall of rock on the right. My first shocked reaction was that it was impossible, but John, carrying the folded chair under his left arm, and with his right arm up the wall, had started along bravely.

When he got to the end, he was wondering how to get down the step from the ledge, when a Dutch lad whom we had met earlier, came back and took the chair from him. There was a second ledge straight after, but it had some plants on the side, which at least gave one a little to hold on to, and the lad gave John a hand getting off; he then came back to help me. I had started out after John, on hands and feet, trying desperately to get some sort of grip. The trouble is that my balance is so dreadful; I can

Narrow and difficult part of the path

wobble and fall backwards on flat ground, let alone a tiny ledge. It was about ten feet long, and seemed like a mile! I discovered later that I'd broken all the nails on my right hand against the rock. When I got to the second ledge, (by this time shaking like a leaf), I was half way along when the Dutch lad came back to hold my arm. After thanking our rescuer, we sat at the edge of the path to recover. I'm afraid I was so shaken by the experience that I burst into tears; I don't think I've ever been more frightened in my life, and we had to wait a while until I stopped shaking!

Shortly afterwards, a chap overtook us who was running. He stopped for a quick word, astounded that we had managed the ledge, and we were equally astounded to find out that he was practicing for an attempt to run the whole Way in twenty four hours. The actual record is apparently sixteen hours.

At Inversnaid, there is the most amazing waterfall, with a bridge right across it. "After the bridge that's the end of walking for you." promised John; but it wasn't by any means; after negotiating some man-made steps down beside the waterfall; there were more steps; then more steps; which I dragged myself down, complaining quite strongly by this point.

We finally came to the Inversnaid Hotel; where we stopped for a couple of well earned pints and chatted to three chaps who were doing the walk. They weren't stopping at Inversnaid, but continuing along the way to the next official stop.

The waterfall at Inversnaid

We said our goodbyes, and started up a very steep hill to the bunk house which was to be our resting place for the night. On the way up, John noticed that the three walkers were following us, and went back to tell them that they were going the wrong way; their way continued along the edge of the loch. They were annoyed that they'd climbed a quarter of the way up the hill unnecessarily, but very grateful that John had gone back to tell them and thus saved them from an even longer trudge; John's good deed for the day.

The bunk house was a converted church with very basic accommodation, but clean and friendly and with a very pleasant atmosphere.

The sleeping rooms were downstairs, with just two small single beds in each. A sleeping bag and pillow were on each bed, and a clean linen envelope which slipped inside the sleeping bag; with a pocket for the pillow; was folded on top, quite a clever idea. There was a shower room for the men, and a separate shower and lavatory for the women, which was at the end of a passage by the back door. The dining room/lounge/bar was upstairs, with the most gorgeous stained glass windows; it also had a fantastic selection of real ales! The people who ran the bunkhouse were very friendly. I'm not sure whether it belonged to them or was run for an organisation, but either way everyone was very pleasant. The chap looked rather hippyish; with longish hair and a beard; one could just imagine him saying "Peace man."

The Bunkhouse at Inversnaid

We had a shower, then went upstairs and sat and drank beer and wrote postcards, we had a very nice meal, and then finished the evening chatting to other walkers. One of the lads had the most awful blisters; in fact his feet were more blister than sole! I felt very sorry for him. He admitted it was his own fault though. Although he and the group he was with were experienced walkers; having done the West Highland Way a couple of times before for charity; he'd bought some new boots in February and hadn't walked them in, fatal. He was going to get the ferry over the loch back to civilisation and leave his mates to carry on.

Stained glass windows of the Bunkhouse

That night my upset tummy reasserted itself for the last time. At approximately 5.30am I had no option but to pay a visit! I had to put on my leg brace and shoes (a bit of a nuisance, but the loo was quite a long way away). There was a walker standing by the back door watching the heavy rain that looked set in for the day, and since I had to pay three visits before breakfast, I found it acutely embarrassing! I was also very worried about how I was going to manage that day's walk, particularly since we'd been told that it was the hardest stretch. As it turned out, my tummy settled down nicely and I had no more bother from it for the rest of the walk.

John received the promised text message from Barbara, and told me that she'd said it was very hard; but considering what we'd already done; we would manage. He later admitted that what she'd also said was that it was a nightmare and even the dog had slipped and nearly fallen into the loch!

Inversnaid to Beinglas Farm (6.5 miles)

After breakfast, at which, amazingly, they provided Earl Grey tea, we donned our waterproofs and set of down the hill to join the Way, which carried on round the loch.

Eating lunch in the rain

Eating crisps in the rain

This was one of the shortest journeys of the trip, only six and a half miles, but as it turned out, it took the longest time, eleven hours.

It was obvious from the start that there was not going to be much riding for me, the path was rocky and narrow and very dangerous for John carrying the chair and the rucksack, as one slip and one could end up falling over the edge and hitting the rocks below. We were passed by many other walkers, some of whom helped us over parts. Two elderly gentlemen picked up the chair and disappeared. We finally found the chair where they had put it down by a gate, about half a mile on, for which we were very grateful, as John was by this time having to make two or three journeys, once with the wheelchair, back for the rucksack, and then sometimes coming back to help me. We were also passed by some people with a man who had a sling on which was obviously new; he looked absolutely dreadful and was quite clearly in a lot of pain. We found out later that he'd fallen and broken his wrist in two places. The poor chap had to finish that section; as there was no way anyone could get to him with transport of any sort; he was then taken by ambulance to a hospital in Glasgow.

The people who passed us were all wishing us well; they were without a doubt very surprised to find us doing the whole walk, and one of the most common comments was "I'll never complain again!" As we approached Rob Roy's cave, the terrain got even steeper. At one point there was a huge natural stone "staircase", which descended about twenty feet. At this point I was exceedingly glad that I'd insisted on taking a rope, because there was no way John could have carried the chair down safely. We tied the rope to the back of the chair, and I sat at the top with my feet braced against rocks and lowered the chair down while John went down backwards holding on to the footrest struts. When he reached the bottom, I threw the rope down and he came back for me. I had to go down backwards with John behind me. A walker took a picture from the bottom for us, but it didn't come out very well as the camera was in a polythene bag to protect it from the rain.

Whilst struggling along the top near the cave, a trip boat went past with the guide giving a commentary about Rob Roy etc. over a loudhailer, he commented on us walkers, and said he thought he'd heard a rude word! At one point he let out a blood curdling scream, and as I was at that time ahead of John and exceedingly worried about his safety; thinking he'd fallen; I nearly fell over the cliff myself.

As we started to move away from the loch, the going began to change. First we came to a gate (where the kind gents had left the wheelchair), then we went along an almost field-like path, where for the first time, I was able to have a short ride. To the left of us were trees, and amongst them, a group of wild black goats. These goats are mentioned in guide books and are quite famous. It is said that they were brought to the area by Rob Roy himself; to provide food for his men.

Wild goats at Loch Lomond side

That relatively smooth bit was very short lived, and the next hurdle we came to was a large wooden ladder, about three feet wide and ten feet high! I climbed up first and pulled the chair up with the rope.

About two and a half miles from the end, we met a young couple from the Czech Republic, who said they'd stay with us and help. They were a Godsend! David, the young man, took it in turns with John to carry either the bag or the chair, and Lucie walked along with me, giving me moral support. We came to a sign saying "Beinglas 2 miles"; someone later commented that a one had fallen off, because it was the longest two miles he had ever walked! After trudging over all sorts of different ground, we came to a hill with a narrow rocky path climbing up and up. My heart dropped into my boots; I was already totally shattered, but David and Lucie came to the rescue. After refusing David's offer of a piggyback! I gratefully accepted when Lucie suggested I hold the loops at the bottom of her rucksack. It worked marvellously; I don't think I'd ever have made it without her. She towed me for literally hours like a broken down car.

David from the Czech Republic

Lucie from the Czech Republic

At times I felt as though I was in a nightmare that I couldn't wake from, but my legs somehow kept moving, although I couldn't stand on my own, and had to keep stopping for a rest. During this part, the wheelchair stuck against a rock and wouldn't move. John gave the jammed chair a hard push and went down on the rock on his shin, poor love, quite a nasty abrasion, but I suppose we were lucky that, together with a much lesser cracked shin for myself, these were the only injuries we suffered.

We wound up and down through woods and heather, and eventually started to see the signs of habitation. Lucie and David left us here, after taking a couple of photos, as they had to get to Glasgow. Our batteries had run down, and because we didn't have the cases, we had been unable to charge any, so David used his camera, and they very kindly sent the pictures through for us on e-mail after returning home. We had intended to make a small detour to a pub called "The Drover's Inn", which apparently is Jimmy Saville's local, but I was so totally exhausted, we just carried on to the hotel; which was actually more of a camp site, with chalets, wigwams and caravans.

I've never been so glad to see habitation in my life! I collapsed into the wheelchair, and John pushed me over the gravel; which only goes to prove how exhausted I was, because I'd never normally expect John

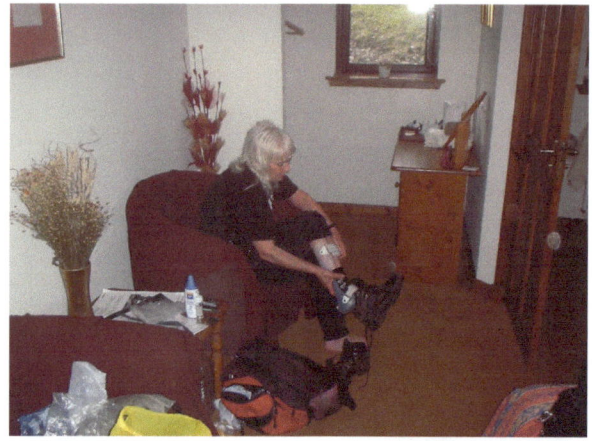

In the chalet at Beinglas Farm

Beingals Farm

Chalet exterior at Beinglas Farm

to push me over gravel, which is extremely hard; as any one used to pushing a wheelchair will verify. Poor John had to go once right round the main building, because we couldn't find the entrance, (which turned out to be a large glass door in an equally large window of one way glass), but we finally crawled into the bar. One of the walkers who had passed us en route held the door open for us, and we went in to a volley of greetings! There were all the people who'd wished us well on the way, glad to see that we'd finally made it. It was 8.15pm and they had just shut the kitchen, but it was opened just for us, and a meal fit for a king was brought out, along with some very welcome beer, which hardly touched the sides on the way down! There were so many chips; I put most of them in a bag for the next day.

We had noticed on route that the rucksack handles were coming apart at the seams, so I'd suggested that we try to get some sewing gear from somewhere. On entering the lovely chalet which we were allocated, what should be on one of the tables, but a mini sewing kit!

BEINGLAS TO CRIANLARICH (6.5 MILES)

Nice sunny day, but we were a little worried by a notice on the way out of the farm, saying that there had been some landslides because of the storm on Thursday night, and to take extra care. I was quite surprised and relieved to find that I felt none the worse for the previous day's ordeal; due, I believe, mainly to June's oils, and John's prowess as a masseur.

We came to a couple of places where water crossed the path and rocks had been washed down from the mountains, but they weren't too bad. The path was pushable for the wheelchair in places, and we followed a rather rough lane past some farm land and decided to stop for a picnic lunch. I ate a few of the cold chips from the evening before, but they were rather dry and not very nice.

We walked under the railway and the A82 and followed them both along for quite a way. For a lot of the West Highland Way, one is following both the railway and the main road, and quite often a river as well.

Moving into wilder country, we were following the old military road, which wasn't too bad, when we came to a section that had been totally chewed up by cattle, and after all the rain of the previous day, was an absolute quagmire with no way round. At this particular point was an engraved notice, thanking some organization for donating the money for the repairs that had been carried out to the road some years before. We had quite a laugh

Climb from Beinglas Farm

Path between Beinglas farm and Crianlarich

Path to Crianlarich

at this considering the state of the place. We emerged at the other side up to our ankles in mud. Luckily, there was a nice little waterfall next to the path, and we sat on a handy rock and washed our footwear. John was wearing his trekking sandals, so his feet got a good wash as well, but rounding a bend in the path, there was another mud section! It was a good thing that there was so much water coming down from the mountain.

We started walking through forest, which was very pretty, but the path was dreadful, very rocky, like large, high cobbles. It was a nightmare with a wheelchair, and there were very few places where I didn't have to walk. Eventually we came to a T junction at a place called Bogle Glen. The Way turned left, but we were going to spend the night at Crianlarich and turned right. The forest track started to drop sharply downwards, and went on for what seemed like miles. The constant cobbles finally proved too much for the gallant wheelchair, and the spokes on one of the little front wheels shattered. Thank goodness we'd brought a spare wheel, lashed to the cross frame with cable ties. It was a matter of minutes to change the wheel, and off we went again, but being a lot gentler with the pushing, because we were now aware that the second small wheel must be feeling the stress as well.

We reached Crianlarich, and stopped at the 'Rod and Reel' for a pint before carrying on to the Ben More Lodge Hotel. Our accommodation again proved to be a chalet, smaller than the last, but really lovely, with chintz curtains and couch cover. We went to the main building for dinner, and I made the mistake of thinking I could match John with a vegetable Phal; phew! Never again!

John gave my legs a good massage, as the constant walking downhill had played havoc with my right thigh. June, the masseuse at the MS drop-in (a weekly meeting for the Stockton MS Group, of which I am a member), had given me a mix of oils for this purpose, and so far they had worked really well; each morning my legs felt fine and the next morning was no exception. However, I was aware that it wouldn't take much to set my thigh off again.

One of John's toes was a little sore from wearing wet sandals, and he decided to wear his boots next day.

Chalet at Ben More Lodge in Crianlarich

Chalet at Ben More Lodge

Chalet exterior

Ben More Lodge main building

Outside our chalet

25

Crianlarich to Bridge of Orchy (13 miles)

The next morning, we exchanged a few words with Quincy, the chef's cat, who was sitting outside the hotel very upset, because he wasn't allowed in when a waitress's Rottweiler was. Very strange I thought, as I'd rather have a small cat near my food than a large smelly Rottweiler.

We took a taxi a couple of miles to join the Way, because neither of us fancied climbing back up the cobbles after what had happened to the wheel the previous day, and we didn't fancy walking along the busy A82. We joined the Way where it crossed the A82, just before a place called Kirkton Farm, which was a camping site with wigwams and a camp shop. It was a fine sunny day, and the going was easy.

Passing by a small lochan, we were intrigued by two carved stones, one on either side of the path. One had a sword carved on it and the other the words 'The legend of the lost sword'. Apparently Robert the Bruce was returning to the hills with some supporters after a defeat at Dalrigh, when they were ambushed and a skirmish ensued. Afterwards the men threw some of their weapons into the lochan to lighten their load before continuing their journey.

We called in at "By the Way" in Tyndrum, which is a camping complex run by a couple of fellow Mensans, whom Chenda, our Mensan leader, had asked us to look up. Mensa is, of course, the previously mentioned club where John and I had first met. We stopped and had a chat with Jim Kinnel; Chenda's friend; then carried on to the hotel for lunch.

Legend of the lost sword

Legend of the lost sword caption

By The Way at Tyndrum

It was warm enough to eat outside, and a couple of beers finished off a very nice meal!

Before carrying on, we stopped at a little general store to buy some more postcards and as it was so sunny, I bought myself a hat. Unfortunately the only hats they had were baseball caps, which I'd sworn I'd never wear, but needs must when the Devil drives and it is very smart, I must admit, royal blue, with "Scotland Forever" emblazoned on the front! I was mightily glad of it during the rest of the walk.

Lunch stop in Tyndrum

Leaving Tyndrum

Tyndrum to Bridge of Orchy

Walking to Bridge of Orchy

The pushing was excellent, so I had quite an easy time of it. Quite a few people passed us and had a chat.

We were going along on a course parallel to and below the railway, when a chap came to meet us. He turned out to be the forest ranger, Mr.Crawford, and he told us that there'd been a landslide from the railway, and we wouldn't get past it. Someone had come to the landslide and had told him that there were some people with a wheelchair coming. We said that we'd come that far, and certainly weren't giving up now, but he was insistent that we couldn't pass. We decided to have a look, and he led

Worsening path on way to Bridge of Orchy

us to it, where there were JCBs and Landrovers and a lot of people milling around, I got the impression that most of the walkers had stayed to see how we'd cope! The bank from the railway had slid down across the path, filling up the whole thing with mud, for about twenty feet. Anyway, as it happened it looked passable to us, it was mainly a matter of climbing up above the mud on the right hand, railway side to go along the top of the slide, which had totally obscured the road. There was a drop on the left side, so that wasn't passable. John went on over the mud with the chair, while Mr. Crawford took the rucksack. I started plodding gingerly through the mud, but it became too deep and I had

to heave myself up about two feet above the mud. With a helping hand from Mr. Crawford, I managed without too much trouble, and with thanks and goodbyes we carried on our way, much relieved that our adventure hadn't been brought to a premature end.

Looking back towards mud slide

View from the train of gang working on the mud slide

Just before we reached Bridge of Orchy, disaster struck! The second wheel broke. This time it was the rim that had broken, and we limped the last bit to the hotel.

By the time we had booked in, I was thoroughly depressed. I simply couldn't see any way out of the situation. John stayed downstairs and tried ringing various places, hospitals etc., to see if anyone could help, and I rang my friend Jenny, who is in a wheelchair and happened to be in Scotland on holiday. Jenny couldn't advise, and neither could the RAC, who were very kind, and tried to help. Eventually, Gilbert from Travel-Lite offered to pick up wheels from Glasgow if John could organize some. By this time it was getting too late to do anything, as everywhere was shut. The hotel room was small and there was nowhere to put the case except the floor. On top of that I'd tried to dry out my very damp diary on the radiator, and it'd slipped down the back and in the ensuing struggle to extricate it, had got very battered; my mood was worsening by the minute! I'd been really looking forward to staying at this hotel, as it was four star, and I was probably expecting too much. I don't think the problems we were having helped either, but I was very disappointed. We decided to leave everything until the morning and went and had dinner, which I must admit was very good, and the service couldn't be faulted.

Nearing Bridge of Orchy

In Bridge of Orchy Hotel

I had tried to get myself used to the idea of having to give up, but tentatively suggested that we try tying cable ties round the wheel on the off chance they may hold the rim together. John jumped at the suggestion, and wrapped a couple round. We did a couple of circuits of the car park and it seemed to hold together. We didn't have many cable ties left, we'd only brought a few to hold the spare wheel on with, so it was quite a decision as to whether it'd be safe to continue, and I was beginning to regret suggesting it.

In the morning, John managed to get hold of the manufacturers of the chair, who gave us the phone number of a wheelchair repairer in Glasgow. John then managed to arrange for some spare wheels to be ready for Gilbert to pick up. Unfortunately the timing meant that we'd have to do two more days walking with the broken wheel. Down in the hotel foyer, the receptionist saw the chair and came out from behind the counter, "Oh!" she exclaimed, "Are you the brave lady who went over the landslide? My husband told me all about you!" It turned out that her husband was Mr. Crawford, the forest ranger who'd helped us! After breakfast, (no Earl Grey tea, just to add to my misery!) as we were about to leave, albeit with reservations as to the wisdom of it, Mrs. Crawford told us that she'd spoken to her husband, and he said that if we got stuck, he'd come and

rescue us! With this in mind, I felt a lot happier about going on, and after promising to let her know when we got safely to the next hotel, off we set.

Bridge of Orchy hotel from the bridge

Bridge of Orchy to King's House (12 miles)

The first part of the walk was great, we went round a hill that could be climbed if one was so inclined (which we weren't!), and came to a pony trekking centre and the Inveroran Hotel. Outside the hotel having a coffee were four of the ladies whom we'd first met at Beinglas Farm (Daphne, Frankie, Taru and Anne). We stopped for a chat and a photo-call, and off we went again.

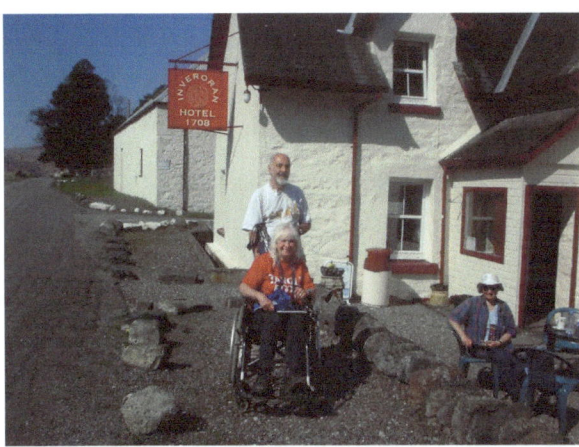

Daphne and friends at Inveroran Hotel for coffee

Outside Inveroran Hotel

The lane started heading towards a forest, but before we got there, we met Mr. Crawford again. He told us to stop at the Forestry Lodge, which was his home, and go to one of the outbuildings and find some more cable ties.

The lodge was right at the start of the forest, which was the end of the good surface and the start of miles of huge cobbles, which are very difficult to take a wheelchair over at the best of times, but when you're nursing a broken wheel, impossible; it was walking time again!

It was while John was finding the cable ties in the outbuilding that Daphne and friends came by. Daphne asked if we'd mind her joining us, as the others were younger than her and liked to keep up a fast pace. I pointed out that we were *very* slow, but she was adamant that she wanted precisely that, so after John had put extra cable ties on the wheel, Daphne joined us whilst the others carried on ahead.

Resting on the way to The King's House

On the path from Inveroran to The Kings House

With Daphne on the path to The King's House

Whilst walking, we kept hearing planes, but although the skies were clear, were unable to see them, which puzzled us.

After a fairly tiring day, walking through beautiful Glencoe, we arrived at a bungalow where Daphne's friends were waiting for her, and continued on to the King's House Hotel, which was a large and very pretty white building standing under a big pointed mountain, called Buachaille Etive Mor, and actually, apart from a few chalet-type bungalows on the road to the hotel; the only building at King's House.

Approaching The King's House

With Daphne and friends in The King's House

The hotel was home to a very fat Newfoundland dog, by the name of Killie, who totally ignored any friendly overtures.

In the passage was a wonderful wooden seat, with the back made from a wagon wheel. It was quite new, and dedicated to a cycling regular, who apparently was a well-known figure with a handlebar moustache, who fed the deer from his hand in the front garden.

Our room was absolutely huge, with the most magnificent view of the mountain and river, glorious!

Dog called Killie at The King's House

View from bedroom window in The King's House

The King's House exterior

View of the Black Mountain from The King's House

Swallows were nesting under the eves, and we tried unsuccessfully to take a photo of them flying past. As I stood looking out of the window in the dusk later, I saw two deer grazing by the water's edge. I was a little piqued the next day to find that they had come right down to the hotel that night, where Daphne and the girls had fed them. They must have been the same ones that the old chap had fed; Daphne said that they were a bit of a disappointment, as they were quite tame and really rather 'moth-eaten' in appearance, obviously very used to walkers feeding them. I finally got round to writing a second lot of postcards, which had been overlooked the previous day due to the disasters!

We added to the wheel some more cable ties that Gilbert had dropped off for us, but unfortunately they weren't strong enough, and broke very quickly; but we still had a few from the forestry lodge.

Kings House to Kinlochleven (9 miles)

The next morning, John decided to wear his sandals again, as his toe seemed to have healed well, and we left Kings House and followed the way towards the infamous Devil's Staircase. Hearing a plane, we turned, and there, following the line of the hills in the valley and almost level with the Way, (which was fairly high up on the right side of the valley, with the range of hills to the left), was a military jet! All the walkers stopped to watch, and we realized that the reason we hadn't been able to see them the previous day, was because they were on the far side of the hill from us.

As we followed the Way along beside the A82, Daphne and friends passed us and stopped for a chat, before heading off in front.

We arrived at the start of the Devil's Staircase, which branched off to the right away from the A82, and climbed up a range of hills and over the top.

Path to The Devil's Staircase

Path to The Devil's Staircase

Crossing a stile near The Devil's Staircase

Drink of water in readiness for the ascent

There were several walkers sitting on rocks at the bottom, resting and charging their batteries ready for the daunting climb, which is a zigzag rocky path about three miles long. Right at the start I slipped and cracked my shin on a rock, but that was the only injury.

Half way up I had my only vertigo attack of the whole walk, but as there was heather beside the track, I was able to lie on my back until my head cleared. Whenever I have an attack, it leaves me feeling a little queasy for a few hours afterwards, and this time was no exception. This is quite a common symptom of MS, and one of the more unpleasant ones.

I wasn't the only one to feel the effects of the climb, however, a young girl had an asthma attack on the way up; I thought she was very brave to have attempted the climb at all, but as soon as the attack passed, she gamely carried on up.

Everyone who passed us congratulated us and wished us well; a couple of favourite phrases were, "I take my hat of to the pair of you!" and "I'll never complain again!" The camaraderie was absolutely fantastic. At one stage we realized that the clip that held one of the footrests in place had fallen off. A chap coming past heard what we were saying, and realized that he'd picked it up earlier and discarded it! He bemoaned the fact that normally he kept anything like that, in case it came in useful, but obviously on the Devil's Staircase, any extra weight was unacceptable; ah well…. We had an amusing encounter too, when; climbing past some teenagers who had stopped for a rest, one of them commented "Ooh, you put us all to shame, walking in sandals"! The fact that John was

Approaching the base of The Devil's Staircase

The base of The Devil's Staircase

Climbing The Devil's Staircase

pushing a wheelchair with a rucksack on it, seemed to have totally escaped her notice; the only thing unusual about us was John's sandals! We giggled about it for quite a while.

I didn't find the Staircase as hard as I was expecting, although I don't think this was because it wasn't hard, I think it was more because I had mentally prepared for it beforehand, and took plenty of rests on the way. Actually, the parts of the whole walk that I found the hardest were the parts that people had told us were easy, so I wasn't prepared for the dreadful surfaces that were impossible for John to push the chair with me in it. We found that what to able-bodied people appeared easy was not at all easy with a wheelchair, so we began to take it with a pinch of salt when people coming the other way told us that the worst was over. One very good thing though, was that my legs were now well "walked in" and I had no more pain with them.

Near the top of The Devil's Staircase

We finally reached the top with some help from two of Daphne's friends, Anne and Taru, who carried the wheelchair for the last little bit, which gave John a bit of respite. The reason they were well behind Daphne and Frankie at this point, was because they had taken a detour up a mountain, and had been playing in the snow!

There were a couple of young Canadians resting at the top as well, and we had our lunch and a good natter before carrying on our way.

It was a five mile walk to Kinlochleven, and it was dreadful; lumpy and uneven, with lots of rocky climbs. We met a lot of interesting people on route, passing us both in our direction, and going the other way. A couple who asked if they could take our photograph, told us that they were physicians from Philadelphia; they said they had a lot of patients who moaned about the tiniest little thing, and wanted to show them our photos because we'd be an 'inspiration' to them! Very flattering!

Daphne's friends at the top of The Devil's Staircase

37

Descent at the other side of The Devil's Staircase

Rough path between The Devil's Staircase and Kinlochleven

There was a group of four people from Holland, who wanted to take our photo to show people at home, and an amusing chap who asked if we would take a photo of him sitting in the wheelchair, so he could show it off in the pub when he got home and everyone would say "How on earth did you get up there in a wheelchair?" Oddly enough, it never occurred to him to ask how on earth WE had got up there with a wheelchair!

My pal Jenny was still in Edinburgh on holiday, and we were texting each other, which was a lovely excuse for a rest every so often, sitting up in the Scottish highlands with a breathtaking view, and making use of modern technology.

We could see Kinlochleven nestling in a valley, and thought it wouldn't be long to go now, but a couple put us right on that misconception. They'd got to the outskirts of the town, and decided to return as it'd taken them a lot longer than planned and they were exhausted. The walk down to Kinlochleven was long, steep, and hugely rocky, as well as being very boring. When we finally got

Adding more cable ties to damaged wheel

to the bottom, it was a very unattractive town, having been the centre of a huge aluminium industry, which was now defunct, but everything was still intact, including four enormous pipes coming down the mountain-side into the town.

We noticed a forest fire burning below us, and wondered how far it would spread. We weren't in the least surprised; as it had been so very dry that the woods were like tinder.

The Macdonald hotel proved to be very nice though, situated on the edge of a sea loch.

We met Daphne and the girls again, although they weren't staying in the hotel, but were in a camping area at the back; however we met in the dining room for dinner later. Daphne said that she'd like to travel with us again the next day, as she'd spent the whole day worrying about us. She was, of course, very welcome, and we arranged to meet outside the hotel in the morning.

When we booked in, we were given our spare wheels which Gilbert had dropped off, but found there were only three. John rang Gilbert, who said the fourth one was in his office and not to worry; he'd get one of the lads to drop it off, which he did. What a relief- whole wheels again, and they were stronger than the original ones. Mind you, the cable ties had worked wonderfully well.

The hotel had vegetarian haggis, which we ordered, with me upsetting Scottish John thoroughly, by asking for salad with mine, when every self respecting Scot knows that one has 'Neaps and Tatties' with haggis! John called me a philistine, but I had the last laugh when the landlord came to say that he was very sorry, but they'd run out of neaps, so John had to have carrots!

John gave me my usual leg massage before retiring, but as I mentioned earlier, my muscles were not anywhere near as sore as they had been, we'd been walking for so long that I'd gone through the muscle pain barrier, and out the other side!

Macdonald Hotel in Kinlochleven

View from Macdonald Hotel

Macdonald Hotel exterior

Kinlochleven to Fort William (14 miles)

During the night, the forest fire had advanced to just the other side of the road outside the hotel, but luckily it had started to rain in the nick of time, much to the relief of the landlord! There were quite large areas of woodland destroyed, but considering how dry everything was, it could have been a lot worse.

We met Daphne outside the hotel, and set off on the last day's journey, which started off with a solid climb for two hours.

Everyone told us that once we'd got to the top, it'd be plain sailing, which was unfortunately only true for the able bodied. The road surface was appalling! We walked along a range of hills, about a quarter of the way up the side, through a valley, and watched a thick mist descending down the mountains. It was getting very cold, and I was very glad of my kagool, and also pleased we had the satellite navigation system with us, in case the mist got right down to our level. In the event, it stopped about half way down and didn't come any further. It was a strange day weather-wise; one minute we were putting waterproofs on and the next stripping them off again because it was too hot.

The road was an old military track, and had the occasional crumbling shepherd's cottage or croft along it, but nowadays the sheep and lambs (of which there were hundreds), were looked after by Landrover. It must

The path out of Kinlochleven

Climbing out of Kinlochleven

Looking back to Kinlochleven

have been a very lonely and bleak existence in the old days, miles from anywhere and at the mercy of the elements. One would have thought that being a used road, the surface would have been at least fair, but attempts had been made to repair and preserve it in its original state, which was OK for sheep and Landrovers, but not so good for wheelchairs! To see it stretching for mile after winding mile in the distance, then to turn round and see the same view behind, was depressing to say the least.

Rough path above Kinlochleven

Rough path from Kinlochleven to Fort William

We could see a forest in the distance, and Daphne had a book with a map in it which indicated an alternative way to Fort William after leaving the forest and we decided to make up our minds later. Meanwhile, some bikes went past followed by a runner. The runner stopped for a chat, and said that the rest of the Way after the forest was pretty tough, with a ladder and some steep climbs, and advised us to take the alternative which, although longer than the official path, was a tarmac road.

We went through the forest, where the road surface was only wheelchair possible (it couldn't by any stretch of the imagination be called friendly!) in places, and when we got to the junction, it was obvious we couldn't get to Fort William before dark at the rate we were going; that, plus the fact that I was absolutely exhausted, and poor Daphne's knees were starting to hurt, caused us to decide to take the smoother route. Even so, it was a long way, and very steep in places, and it still took us a couple more

Near Lundavra

41

hours. We had a good view of the great Ben Nevis all the way, and stood at the top looking down onto Fort William with relief.

First view of Fort William

First view of Ben Nevis

It was about 8.30pm when we reached the finishing post, and after taking some photos by the sign, we said our goodbyes to Daphne and she went off to her hotel which was back the way we'd come a bit, and we went into ours, which was called The Nevis Bank Hotel, and was right next to the finishing post.

Daphne at the end of The West Highland Way

Us at the end of The West Highland Way

We decided that it was too late to have our usual shower and change before dinner, so I said I'd just change my jeans. I took off my leg brace and turned round to get my clean jeans, and promptly went over on my ankle and landed up a heap on the floor! My foot went purple just above my little toe, and I was convinced I'd broken the metatarsal. I strapped it up as tightly as I could, and we went to the reception desk for advice. We were told to go to the local hospital, which we'd passed on the way to the hotel, and was only about a five minute walk away. Knowing we'd miss dinner if we went first, we opted to have a meal and then go. The doctor at the accident and emergency also thought my foot might be broken, as by that time there was a swelling like an egg near my ankle. However, the radiologist couldn't get there until the next morning, so they strapped me up firmly and sent us away.

Breakfast at The Nevis Bank Hotel

At breakfast the next morning, an American lady came over to ask if we were the couple who's just done the Way, and congratulated us when we said we were. After breakfast, we went back to the A and E for an x-ray, which thank goodness showed no break. I was told to keep off my foot (good thing we had a wheelchair!), and we went back to the hotel with just enough time for a coffee before getting a taxi to the station.

Fort William Accident & Emergency Department

We were seen off by a lady who congratulated us, wishing us all the best, and the taxi driver, bless him, when he found out we'd just done the West Highland Way, refused to take a fare, telling us to put it towards our charity.

Nevis Bank Hotel exterior

43

The train journey followed the path we'd walked, right to Loch Lomond, where it went round the other side. I didn't see much of John on the first part, as he was galloping from side to side of the carriage taking photos!

We saw the workmen on the path below repairing the area where the landslide had been. It was fascinating seeing it from above, and interesting to see how much work they'd done since we were there.

We were talking to some passengers during the journey, and told them we'd just completed the walk, when a young chap further down the carriage said he'd heard all about us, and well done for finishing. Then at Edinburgh station, three chaps who had done the walk said we were wonderful, but considering it had only taken them three days, I thought they were the ones who were wonderful! Anyway, I got a kiss from each of them, which was very nice!

When we got to our platform, we got chatting to the manageress of GNER at Edinburgh, who I think was called Karen, who told us she was leaving Edinburgh to move to Berwick. We told her about our walk and how I'd hurt my foot after finishing it. She was quite horrified when we said there was no assistance at Billingham, as it was an unmanned station, and there was a bridge with a lot of steps to cross. We assured her that we'd manage, but she asked for the tickets, and went off chatting on the phone. At that point the train came in, and she gave us back the tickets, and up the ramps we went. After we were settled nicely on the train, and it was on the way, a woman with a GNER badge came up and asked if I had a mobile phone, as someone from the office wanted to phone us. We gave her John's number, and away she went. Shortly afterwards, the phone rang, and it was Karen, who told John she had organized a taxi for us, to take us all the way from Newcastle, which was where we were supposed to get the Billingham train, to home! The phone went again, and a chap from Newcastle, who insisted on talking to me personally, rang to confirm the arrangement! Well, we were absolutely amazed; it was a very long way! When we got to Newcastle, sure enough there was a taxi for us, a London type cab, but in almost psychedelic livery! The taxi driver was a friendly soul, who told us that GNER always used him if there was a problem at a station that was their fault. We pointed out that it wasn't their fault at all, we'd known that the station had a bridge when we booked, and it certainly wasn't their fault that I'd hurt my foot, but he said that they would consider it their responsibility. What a wonderful service, GNER deserve a medal!

When we reached home, John put the rucksack by the front gate and turned round to help me out, when a teenager on a bike came flying up the pavement at a ridiculous speed and knocked him flying backwards into the taxi, hitting his head on the open door. I was so upset I yelled at the kid, calling him all the idiots under the sun, whilst John was assuring him that he was fine, and asking if HE was alright! John reckoned I was more upset than he, but I've been expecting this sort of accident for ages, and he could have been badly hurt.

HOME AGAIN!

Euphoria! I was on a high for several weeks after getting back; it took a long time to come down to earth again. At night I even dreamt I was walking ………… plod, plod, plod.

We were delighted to raise over £800 for the Stockton MS group, for which we say a big thank you to all those who sponsored us.

So to sum up, I wouldn't advise anyone to try what we did, it was very dangerous, but I don't regret it for a moment. To those able bodied people, who say "I couldn't do it", bear in mind that John and I are no spring chickens, we were both rising 64 when we began our great adventure, and I have MS, so never say "I can't"; it's amazing what one can accomplish with determination, or sheer bloody mindedness.

Epilogue

Since finishing the walk, we have acquired a 'Musmate', which is a harness with an elastic band which goes over the shoulder and is attached to the walking boot of the weak leg. This is an amazing gadget, being very simple but very efficient. We have also bought an amazing newly designed 'off road' wheelchair, called a 'Trekinetic'. Huge mountain bike tyres at the front, and one smaller wheel with suspension at the rear, makes this like no other wheelchair. It also has handlebars for pushing with drum brakes. On top of this, I have a little gadget called a 'Shewee', which I will only say makes private moments a lot more private!

If we had had all these new innovations on the big walk, they would have made a terrific difference to some of the harder parts of the journey.

In 2007 we have planned to do the continuation of the walk, which is called the Great Glen, and travels from Fort William to Inverness, across from west to east.

<u>The End</u>